# PHILOSOPHERS DO EXIST

## *This is for The People*

JAMIE DAVIS

**author**HOUSE®

*AuthorHouse™*
*1663 Liberty Drive*
*Bloomington, IN 47403*
*www.authorhouse.com*
*Phone: 833-262-8899*

*Published by AuthorHouse  10/19/2022*

*ISBN: 978-1-6655-7346-7 (sc)*
*ISBN: 978-1-6655-7345-0 (e)*

*Print information available on the last page.*

*This book is printed on acid-free paper.*

# ACKNOWLEDGEMENT

THE DAVIS FAMILY, THE HILL FAMILY, THE HOWARD FAMILY, THE PATTERSON FAMILY, THE BARNETT FAMILY, THE ADAMS FAMILY, DIGBY AND THE WILLIAMS FAMILY, THE MEMPHIS DAVIS FAMILY, THE ATLANTA DAVIS FAMILY, AND THE ENTIRE DAVIS FAMILY ALL AROUND, MARK COGIC CHURCH AND FAMILY, REDEEM MINISTRIES, MORGAN PARK CHURCH MINISTRIES, CHRISTIAN CONCEPTS INTERNATIONAL MINISTRIES, KOINDA NETWORK, JEWEL OSCO FAMILY, FACEBOOK FAMILY AND FRIENDS, GINA RAGLAND AND GRACE, ROBERT AND SHARON HOLMES, KAREN MUNRO, SEARCY LOVETT, TAKESHA HOWARD AND FAMILY, AND TO ALL THAT MIGHT NOT BE MENTIONED BUT NOT FORGOTTEN MUCH LOVE. AND SPECIAL DEDICATIONS TO MY LOVING BIG SISTER SISTER LINDA CAROL DAVIS YOU ARE THE FEW SISTERS THAT MADE ME REALLY LAUGH AND WE ENJOYED YOUR AMAZING SINCE OF HUMOR AND TO THE LATE APOSTLE LANCER DELASHMENT GONE TO SOON BUT INSPIRE ME FOR A LIFE TIME.

# PHILOSOPHER

A kind of person that sees the world differently than everybody else. They are sometimes misunderstood, due to the fact that they could break the spirit of those near them. There are a lot of people who do not like philosophers. Some try to disprove their beliefs. But philosophers just want to have an understanding of everything. They look at all angles of any given situation. They judge fairly in all things.

To be a philosopher is to lift the weights of the mistakes here on Earth. And to willingly go down along with that burden. They do this for people, for you. They question the things that nobody wants to question. They are frank at times but true. So next time, if you meet someone that fits that description, do not look at him or her with annoyance. Greet that someone and make a great conversation. Ask for their wisdom. There may be times that you do not agree with them but I tell you, they don't also like what comes out of their mouths sometimes.

1| "WHAT BRINGS ONE DOWNPLAYS A MAJOR ROLE IN WHAT LAUNCHES ONE HIGHER."(JD) the philosopher "LIFE IS ABOUT FIGURING IT OUT!"(JD) the philosopher

— *I wrote this inspired by not being chosen for a group that I wanted to belong too but after 3 weeks gone by, I was insulted that I was not chosen and hurt but very inspired to rise and prove to them that I'm a writer and a philosopher.*

2| "IT IS SAID, NEVER UNDERESTIMATE THE HEART OF A CHAMPION BUT THAT HEART MAY BEAT IN ONE YOU LEAST EXPECT"(JD) the philosopher

3| "LIFE IS ABOUT FIGURING IT OUT!"(JD) the philosopher

4| "EVERY GREAT ONE FACED AND HAVE FACED CHALLENGES THAT HAVE MADE THEM QUESTION THEMSELVES!"(JD) the philosopher

5| "WHEN ONE'S VISION CAN SEE THE BIGGER PICTURE AND NOT THE BIGGER PURSE, THAT IS WHEN ONE TRULY HAS REAL SIGHT"(JD) the philosopher

— *I wrote this inspired by, having a vision is greater than how much I make in capital gain and status.*

6| "FACING YOUR FEARS WILL EITHER SHOW HOW TUFF THEY ARE OR PROVE HOW WEAK THEY REALLY ARE"(JD) the philosopher.

— *I wrote this inspired by understanding things we fear are not as bad as we feel and if we face them, we can prove they are just our Imagination.*

7| "WHAT ONE SEE AS IMPERFECTION, ANOTHER SEE AS A MASTERPIECE."(JD)the philosopher

— *I wrote this believing that beauty in the eye of the beholder.*

8| "TRUE GENIUS IS BIRTHED OUT OF PASSION OVER PRIDE"(JD)the philosopher

9| "IF YOU WANT SOMETHING DIFFERENT. DO SOMETHING DIFFERENT!"(JD) the philosopher

— *I wrote this to those that believe that insanity is doing the same thing over again but expecting a different result so let's change it up.*

|10| "YOU GET BETTER THREW EXPERIENCE "(GIANNIS ANTEOKWNMPO)

|11| "SOMETIMES WHEN YOU GAVE IT ALL YOU HAD, NOW ITS TIME TO OFFER WHAT YOU DON'T HAVE!"(JD) the philosopher

|12| "PURE GOLD SHOULD NEVER DESIRE TO BE POLISHED SILVER IN ALL ITS GLORY"(JD) the philosopher

|13| "All men are not liar's; some are inaccurate based off the info they were given."(JD) the philosopher

|14| "HEARING ON TIME AND BEING HEARD ON TIME IS EVERYTHING!"(JD) the philosopher)

15| "WE ARE MADE IN HARDNESS!" (JESSIE M DIGBY

— *I wrote this threw what was quoted to me by my aunt like the golden saying that helps us understand that trials make people stronger in life.*

16| ) "I DON'T BELIEVE IN REINVENTING BUT I BELIEVE ONE HAS HEIGHTS AND DEPTHS OF ONE SELF THAT IS UNDISCOVERED."(JD) the philosopher

17| "IT IS SAID, NEVER UNDERESTIMATE THE HEART OF A CHAMPION BUT THAT HEART MAY BEAT IN ONE YOU LEAST EXPECT"(JD) the philosopher

18| "WHEN ONE'S VISION CAN SEE THE BIGGER PICTURE AND NOT THE BIGGER PURSE, THAT IS WHEN ONE TRULY HAS REAL SIGHT"(JD) the philosopher

19| "FACING YOUR FEARS WILL EITHER SHOW HOW TUFF THEY ARE OR PROVE HOW WEAK THEY REALLY ARE"(JD) the philosopher

20| "WHAT ONE SEE AS IMPERFECTION, ANOTHER SEE AS A MASTERPIECE."(JD)the philosopher

21| "TRUE GENIUS IS BIRTH OUT OF PASSION OVER PRIDE"(JD)the philosopher

22| "IF YOU WANT SOMETHING DIFFERENT, DO SOMETHING DIFFERENT!"(JD) the philosopher

23| "YOU GET BETTER THREW EXPERIENCE "(GIANNIS ANTEOKWNMPO)

24| "SOMETIMES WHEN YOU GAVE IT ALL YOU HAD, NOW ITS TIME TO OFFER WHAT YOU DON'T HAVE!"(JD) the philosopher

25| "PURE GOLD SHOULD NEVER DESIRE TO BE POLISHED SILVER IN ALL ITS GLORY"(JD) the philosopher

— *I wrote this about when you are authentic in character never desire to be someone else but cherish your uniqueness because it will show.*

26| "HEARING ON TIME AND BEING HEARD ON TIME IS EVERYTHING!"(JD) the philosopher)

27| "BEING FAMILIAR IS EASY AND BEING DIFFERENT IS HARD BUT BEING HEARD IS DEVINE!"(JD) the philosopher

28| "YOUR LIFE IS A REFLECTION OF YOUR DECISIONS!"(SHUELER KING)

29| "IF I HAD YOUR HAND, I WOULD THROW MINES AWAY!"(URBAN CITY PHILOSOPHY)

— *I wrote this in remembrance of hearing quoted in the urban community I grew up in by some of the coolest men you could run into about wishing and admiring where you are in comparison to them just walking down the street as a greeting.*

30| "THERE ARE PEOPLE I LOVE, THEN THERE ARE PEOPLE I JUST LIKE!"(Cody Vernon Marshall)

— *I wrote this in hearing it quoted by a great man on the microphone about your choice of special people you like in comparison to people you love overall.*

31| "Never base friendship on only those that celebrate you and enemies on only those that don't congratulate you" (Eugene Fears Jr)

— *I wrote this and will give you the original word that was said by a great speaker over the microphone and it was said (everybody that pat you on your back aren't your friend, and just because I don't pat you on your back all the time doesn't mean I'm not your true friend.)*

32| "THOSE WHO DO NOT REMEMBER THE PAST ARE CONDEMNED TO REPEAT IT" (George Santayana)

33| "EVERY KISS IS NOT ALWAYS A SHOW OF LOVE "(JD) the philosopher.

— *I wrote this in remembrance of Jesus interaction with his betrayer and people that are not genuine in their motives and affections.*

34| AS OUR SOULS DESCEND BACK INTO OUR MORTAL FORM, AS WE CRADLE EACH OTHER UNTIL THE RISING OF THE MORNING SUN (Mary Pipkins)

35| THE EASIEST THING TO DO IS TO GIVE UP, BUT THE HARDEST PART IS TO FIGHT - (DRIQ WRITE)

36| The worst part of sharing your feelings is sharing your feelings to a person who don't care about how you feel.
DRIQ WRIGHT

37| "THE THING THERE IS NO ANSWER FOR, THERE SHOULD BE NO QUESTION"(JD) the philosopher

38| "THERE IS BEAUTY IN MISTAKES!"(JD)the philosopher

— *I wrote this after seeing video of the superstar funkster George Clinton account of what mistakes that happen in the studios of drum tracks that were played backward and his intoxication while recording that was a mess at best but produced the hit song (Atomic Dog)*

39| "TO TRULY OVERCOME IS TO TAKE BACK, WHAT WAS ONCE TAKEN"(JD) the philosopher

— *I wrote this as a person experiencing challenges with a disease, I battle but have rallied back to reclaim my life that was crazy for awhile with love and support from beautiful people that cared*

40| "TRUE CONFLICT IS WHEN ONE LOOSES CONTROL OVER THE ONCE CONTAINED"(JD) the philosopher

— *I wrote this once again about the conflicts that I faced and still face battling a disease and ambiguous to those that can understand.*

41| "WE WILL SELL NO WINE BEFORE ITS TIME"(PAUL MASSON)

42| "EASE IS A GREATER THREAT TO PROGRESS THAN HARDSHIP"(DENZEL WASHINGTON)

43| "THE TEST SEEDS OF HUMILITY ARE OFTEN SOWN WITH HUMILIATION BUT BRINGS FORTH HONOR"(JD) the philosopher

— *I wrote this in seeing an incident that transpired during the 2022 Oscars with a comedian and a Oscar award winner that left me stunned but made me have the greatest respect for one that I believe showed character that was praise worthy and of honor.*

44| "THAT WAS THE GREATEST NIGHT IN THE HISTORY OF TELEVISION."(CHRIS ROCK)

45| "JUST CAUSE YOU'RE CORRECT DON'T MEAN YOU'RE RIGHT!"(COMEDIAN SHUELER KING)

46| "TO HOLD ONE'S PEACE WILL CREATE A BETTER OPPORTUNITY TO BE HEARD GREATER" (JD) the philosopher

— *I wrote this once again about what transpired at the Oscar awards that though it was embarrassing prove to many that holding your peace comes to pay off when you have patience.*

47| "Never risk it all, especially when there is nothing to gain."(MARCELLUS WILEY)

48| "ALWAY'S REMEMBER YOU ARE A WALKING CANVAS OF SOMEONE'S CREATION."(JD) the philosopher

49| "Just like anything can go wrong, Somethings can go Right!"(JD) the philosopher

50| "THE HARDER THE CONFLICT, THE SWEETER THE TRIUMPH"(THOMAS PAINE)

51| "YOU FIRST HAVE TO DIG DEEP IF YOU WANT TO RISE HIGH!"(JD) the philosopher

52| "DESIRED IS NOT ALWAYS DESERVED AND DESERVED IS NOT ALWAYS DESIRED."(JD) the philosopher

53| "THE BEST KIND OF EXPERIENCE IS TO BE INVOLVED AND INVESTED."(JD) the philosopher

54| "YOU DON'T UNDERSTAND ONE'S POSSIBILITIES UNTIL YOU KNOW ONE'S CAPABILITIES."(JD) the philosopher

55| "LIMITED CHOICES CAN ALSO TRANSLATE INTO LIMITED MISTAKES."(JD) the philosopher

56| "THE DIFFERENCE IN MAKING FRIENDS AND BUILDING ALLIANCES IS MOTIVE AND PURPOSE."(JD) the philosopher

— *I wrote this in seeing that some were not honest in friendship only to get support of questionable character and flawed person while others are genuine and without motive.*

57| "The thing about it is: if we don't make a decision about us, somebody else gone make a decision about us!"(AB burns Tucker)

58| "IF IT AIN'T BROKE DON'T FIX IT! "(Thomas Bertram Lance)

59| "NEVER COMPLICATE SIMPLICITY!"(JD) the philosopher

60| "ONE'S TRIVIA OF COMPLEX, TELLS ALOT ABOUT ONE'S ATTRACTION AND DESIRES THAN THE COMPLEXITY"(JD) the philosopher

61| "WHEN THERE IS NO REAL CLOSURE: THERE IS NO TRUE PEACE!"(JD) the philosopher

62| "SOME LIVE OFF THE WHAT IF? AND YOU DON'T GET CLOSURE, AND IF YOU DON'T GET REAL CLOSURE, YOU DON'T GET PEACE!"(JD) the philosopher

63| "I THINK THAT FACE BOOK IS THE BUSINESSMAN: IF YOU USE IT TO YOUR FUNCTION"(JD) the philosopher

64| "LOVE IS MOST! THE INVISIBLE MAN YET NEAR YOU HEAR, THOUGH I (DISAPPEAR!)"(JD) the philosopher from excerpts of poem (DISAPPEAR)

65| "I'M An ARTSY, COLORFUL, INSPIRATIONAL, THOUGHT PROVOKING PHILOSOPHER!"(JD) the philosopher

66| "YOU CANNOT PREPARE OR CONTROL THE TRUTH."(ESPERENZA SPALDING)

67| "SOMETIMES HONESTY WILL EXPOSE YOUR TRUE FLAWS BUT IT WILL ALSO SHOW YOUR TRUE HEART"(JD) the philosopher

— *I wrote this concerning me being able to admit that I have a disease that meant being honest means being exposed but with it you get an opportunity to see me uncovered and my heart which is my best strength.*

68| "I DON'T WANNA CARRY SOMEONES ELES'S MESSAGE, IF IT HURTS OR DESTROY OTHERS"(JD) the philosopher

69| "IT'S ABOUT IMPACT!"(SINQUA WALL)

70| "THE MIRACLE IS NOT IN THE METHOD; THE MESSAGE IS IN THE MIRACLE"(JD) the philosopher

71| "GIVE FROM THE BAG OF ONE'S BEST AND MAKE A PRESENTATION THAT WILL LIVE BEYOND ONE'S APPEARANCE"(JD) the philosopher

72| "PURE GOLD IS MENT TO BE FOUND NOT PURCHASED BECAUSE OF THE JOURNEY ADDS VALUE AND WORTH"(JD) the philosopher

— *I wrote this concerning the misconception that a young minister giving an example of a miracle of Jesus to a watching audience that backfired because he led with what method Jesus used which was not sanitary to say the least but did fail to mention that his method was not the point but his message which was overlooked.*

73| "A LETTER TO A WORD, A WORD TO A SENTENCE, A SENTENCE TO A QUOTE, AND QUOTE TO A MESSAGE"(JD) the philosopher

74| "WHAT ENTERTAINS ONE, INSULTS ANOTHER, WHAT ELAVATES ONE, BRINGS DOWN ANOTHER"(JD) the philosopher

75| "SOMETIMES WHEN ONE IS BLEEDING, NO ONE CAN SEE IT"(JD) the philosopher

76| "LIVE IN THE MOMENT, BECAUSE IT'S THERE WHERE THE MAGIC HAPPENS!"(JD) the philosopher

77| "IF YOU ARE NOT REACHABLE, YOU ARE NOT A (BIRD IN THE HAND)"(JD) the philosopher

78| "WHEN YOU LIVE IT, YOU ARE NOT CONSCIENCE OF THE INFLUENCES OF WHERE IT'S COMING FROM"(ESPENZA SPAULDING)

— *I wrote this concerning people not seeing value in their character because it doesn't bring them notice but forget that their authenticity is pure and will give the best value to them not their display of ego.*

79| "As much as one has to care to trust, one also must trust to care"(JD) the philosopher

80| "I'm good enough to succeed, but I'm human enough to fail."(JD) the philosopher

— *I wrote this showing that no matter how flawless we may look we make a lot of mistakes that shows at our best we are still human and subject to flaws and great mistakes.*

81| "All retaliation is not counter justice but in time certain justice!"(JD) the philosopher

82| "NOBODY IS NOBODY!"(JD) the philosopher

83| "I RATHER EAT CRUMBS WITH BUMS, THAN EAT STEAKS WITH SNAKES!"(THE MOB)

84| "HUMILITY IS THE PRICE ONE PAY'S IN ROUTE TO REACH TRUE DESTINY."(JD) the philosopher

85| "Why? does some doors need to be open when one has the key."(JD) the philosopher

86| "SOMETIMES ONE HAS TO STOP THINKING TO ENJOY!"(JD) the philosopher

87| "After difficulty comes ease and we don't get the ease by ducking the difficulty."(BEN X)

88 | "SOMETIMES BEING OVERCONFIDENT CAN BE ONE'S MOST SURPRISING FAILURE."(JD) the philosopher

89 | "Put down your phones, your text, your emails will be there later the person in front of you will not."(TINY BUDDHA)

90 | "DON'T BE SOMETHIN ANYBODY CAN BE, BE SOMETHIN ANYBODY CAN'T BE!"(HUBERT CREDIT)

— *This was said by the great late minister in explaining the importance of being unique and being special and not following the crowds.*

91 | "PEOPLE HAVE A RIGHT TO An OPINION, AND THEY ALSO HAVE A RIGHT TO BE WRONG!"(JD) the philosopher

92 | "WHEN YOU'VE RUN OUT OF CHOICES, YOU HAVE TO BE BRAVE ENOUGH TO TAKE RISK."(JD) the philosopher

93 | "When one shed's blood it's a sign one is truly human."(JD) the philosopher

94 | "Disappointment is one appointment that when faced will make one better."(JD) the philosopher

95 | "FEAR IS A GOOD INDICATOR OF WHAT ONE BELIEVES"(JD)

96| "THERE IS NO CONFUSION IN AUTHENTICITY."(JD) the philosopher

97| "Like many creatures snakes do retreat, but snakes don't take orders."(JD) the philosopher

98| "NEVER TRY TO OUTRUN YOUR REALITY! BECAUSE IT WILL CATCH UP WITH YOU EVERYTIME."(JD) the philosopher

— *I wrote this concerning being true to oneself and appreciating and accepting you mistakes, success, flaws, because it is the side of us that we can't escape but helps us to grow.*

99| "Running from reality is a self-inflicted wound."(JD) the philosopher

100| One of the side effects of (you know!) messing with drugs, you always feel like somebody is doing something to you."(G CLINTON)

101| "There are some wound's that come with the (game's one play) and some with the game that (play's one),"(JD) the philosopher

102| "I feel for one's wounds that were inflicted and not self-inflicted."(JD) the philosopher

103| "Generally, where there is a lot of rules, there is not a lot of love."(RICHARD DANIEL HENTON)

104| "I ain't Gott 'a explain what's understood!"(DEONTAY WILDER)

105| When One's kindness is memorable, then One's smile is UNFORGETTABLE! (JD) the philosopher

106| "One that has truly paid dues has earned the right to be honest."(JD) the philosopher

— *I wrote this concerning the former NBA player Scottie Pippen that caught a lot of smoke from critics concerning his novel (UNGUARDED) where he was criticized for being honest about the things that happen during his time playing for the Chicago Bulls organization and criticism of a person people praised as the G.O.A.T in game where he viewed it as a team's game and not a individual's game.*

107| "(SUCCESS!) IT'S GOT ENEMIES."(AMERICAN GANGSTER)

108| "THE WORST BETRAYEL IN THE WORLD IS FALSE INTIMACY."(TD JAKES)

109| "You don't control trust; you have confidence in trust."(JD) the philosopher

110| "IF NO ONE IS TALKING ABOUT YOU, ITS PROBABLY BECAUSE YOU AIN'T DOING NOTHING."(BILLY RAY CYRUS)

111| "MAKE LIFE INTERESTING FOR YOU!"(JD) the philosopher

112| "IT TOOK ME AWHILE TO REALIZE THAT THE AMERICAN DREAM IS NOT FOR ALL OF US."(TIMOTHY WARD)

|113| "CALLING OUT THE DEVIL IS ONE THING, FACING HIM IS ANOTHER."(KENDALL GILL)

|114| "YOU DON'T HAVE TO TELL YOUR STORY, TIME WILL!"(CANDACE PARKER)

|115| HOW IS YOUR HAPPY HEALTH? (JD) the philosopher

|116| "ANCIENT WISDOMS HELP SHAPE A COUNTRY'S MODERN-DAY CULTURE MORE THAN WE MAY REALISE."(EDIRA PUTRI)

|117| "Truth will always Trump the facts because the facts reveal, but the Truth Fulfills"(JD) the philosopher

|118| "TO ATTEMPT IS THE ROAD TO SUCCESS.!"(JD) the philosopher

|119| "PEOPLE WHO TAKE CHANCES, THESE ARE THE ONLY PEOPLE YOU CAN TRUST."(EVANDER HOLYFIELD)

|120| "A GREAT WINNER IS JUDGED BY HOW HE LOSES."(ROY JONES JR)

|121| " SOMETIMES YOU HAVE TO WAIT FOR SOME FIRES TO CATCH ON, TO REALLY GRILL!"(JD) the philosopher

|122| "SOME CRITICS ARE SECRET ADMIRERS IN DISGUISE."(JD) the philosopher

|123| "ONE'S LIMITATIONS ARE ALWAYS BASED ON ONE'S LIMITED UNDERSTANDING."(JD) the philosopher

|124| "Allow the light to right the wrongs in your life and explain the unexplainable in your world"(JD) the philosopher

|125| "50/50 is a partnership, 90/10 is Employment." (PRINCE)

|126| "Never sell one's soul for desperate gains, because the evil buyer doesn't issue refunds on a shady deal."(JD) the philosopher

|127| "With Wickedness comes Severe Consequences but with Righteousness comes Great Opportunities"(JD) the philosopher

|128| "Know the horse in the race and not the race."(JD) the philosopher

129| "YOU HAVE TO HAVE YOUR FINGER ON THE PULSE OF ONE ABILITY YOUR EXCELLENCE CAN EXPLOIT!"(JD) the philosopher

130| "SOME WHERE IN THE THINGS ONE FEAR IS BELIEF."(JD) the philosopher

— *I wrote this concerning the reality of how we process our true fears that ties back to False fears we believe in that is not proven to have merit accept in our minds.*

131| "WHEN THE SIMPLE DESIRES TO FIT IN, THE CALLED ARE CHOSEN TO STAND OUT."(JD) the philosopher

— *I wrote this out of my personal jealousy of people desiring to fit in what is common and not praising their uniqueness.*

132| "POWER TALKS TO POWER!"(JD) the philosopher

133| "WHEN IT IS YOUR TIME TO BE GREAT, TAKE ADVANTAGE OF IT AND BE GREAT!

134| "(JD) the philosopher

135| "YOU HAVE TO LET GO, LET GO OF EVERYTHING AND REMEMBER YOU ARE NOT THE SHARPEST KNIFE IN THE DRAWER."(MICHAEL K WILLIAMS)

136| "THE PERSON MANY EXPERIENCES IN YOU NOW, IS THE LOVE ALREADY IN PROGRESS BETWEEN YOU AND THE LIGHT."(JD) the philosopher

137| "PAINT THE HONEST SOLUTION IN THE COLORS OF ENCOURAGEMENT."(JD) the philosopher

138| "IT TOOK ME AWHILE TO REALIZE THAT THE AMERICAN DREAM IS NOT FOR ALL OF US."(TIMOTHY WARD)

139| "ANCIENT WISDOMS HELP SHAPE A COUNTRY'S MODERN-DAY CULTURE MORE THAN WE MAY REALISE."(EDIRA PUTRI)

140| "Truth will always Trump the facts because the facts reveal, but the Truth Fulfills"(JD) the philosopher

141| "WHEN THE SIMPLE DESIRES TO FIT IN, THE CALLED ARE CHOSEN TO STAND OUT."(JD) the philosopher

142| "A FIST ALWAYS UNITES THE HAND."(JD) the philosopher

> — *I wrote this concerning the concept of unity that even plays out in our anatomy and the showing what one can do when there is unity and togetherness.*

143| "EVERY GREAT ONE FACED AND HAVE FACED CHALLENGES THAT HAVE MADE THEM QUESTION THEMSELVES!"(JD) the philosopher

144| "WHEN ONE'S VISION CAN SEE THE BIGGER PICTURE AND NOT THE BIGGER PURSE, THAT IS WHEN ONE TRULY HAS REAL SIGHT"(JD) the philosopher

145| "Never let one's rain ruin one's sunshine."(JD) the philosopher

146| "This is not the time to create a problem but to be a part of the solution."(JD) the philosopher

147| "The beauty of truth begins when the mirror of denial ends."(JD) the philosopher

148| "All problems are not meant to be solved but rather heard."(JD) the philosopher

149| "The art of love is like baseball; you have to threw out the first pitch."(JD) the philosopher

150| "A GOOD MAN'S THOUGHT'S MAY FADE, BUT HIS LOVE NEVER WILL."(JD) the philosopher

|51| "One whom walk's the path of the wise is never lost, just on a journey."(JD) the philosopher

|52| "Get busy living or get busy dying."(SHAWSHANK REDEMPTION)

|53| "A WISE MAN ONCE SAID, YOU HAVE TO LET A MAN FIND HIS BALANCE."(JD) the philosopher

|54| "TO PLAN IS NOT FOR LOOSING, TO HOPE IS NOT FOR FAILURE AND TO WISH IS NOT FOR A BAD DAY."(JD) the philosopher

|55| "Giants do fall and once walkers now crawl, and ill winds blow away."(JD) the philosopher

|56| "It's always great to have more than enough but sometimes less is more."(JD) the philosopher

|57| "KNOW YOUR REALITIES, PROMISES, AND BOUNDARIES BUT NEVER LIMIT YOURSELF."(JD) the philosopher

|158| "THE ONLY THING WORSE THAN BEING TALKED ABOUT IS NOT BEING TALKED ABOUT." (PHINEAS T BARNUM)

|159| "THE GIFT THAT WARMS A HEART, CHILLS ANOTHER."(JD) the philosopher

|160| WHAT ONE HAS IS NOT IN DEMAND BY THOSE UNAWAYER OF THE'RE NEEDS."(JD) the philosopher

|161| ONE IS NEVER WITHOUT GIFTS, JUST WHAT ONE HAS IS NOT IN DEMAND BY THOSE UNAWAYER OF THE'RE NEEDS."(JD) the philosopher

— *I wrote this concerning people that feel not important and insignificant but overlook that you are significant its just what you have has to come into desire and it makes you even more valuable.*

|162| "WHAT ONE SEE AS IMPERFECTION, ANOTHER SEE AS A MASTERPIECE."(JD)the philosopher

— *I wrote this concerning beauty being in the eye of the beholder and genius is left up to the individual.*

|163| "Being young is really not a excuse for ignorance." (WILLIE D)

|164| "BECOME WHO YOU ARE CREATED TO BE!"(JD) the philosopher

|165| "A GOOD MAN'S LOVE IS NEVER FOR SALE, ITS FREE! YOU DON'T EARN IT, YOU RECEIVE IT."(JD) the philosopher

|166| "LIES ARE FOR SALE BUT THE TRUTH IS FREE."(JD) the philosopher

|167| DON'T ASK MY NEIGHBOR, AND NEVER ASK THE FRIENDS I HANG AROUND, COME TO ME."(THE EMOTIONS)

|168| "In life there has to be balance because win's build our hope and loses build our integrity."(JD) the philosopher

|169| "One has to start because if you don't start you can't finish."(JD) the philosopher

— *I wrote this concerning starting is motion and motion is a start to finish and leave everything finished is the goal.*

|170| "ANY WISE PHILOSOPHER KNOW THE IMPORTANCE OF WORDS BECAUSE THEY WILL GO ON TO OUT LIVE THEM."(JD) the philosopher

|171| "Cry about it today and laugh at it tomorrow" or "Laugh at it today and Cry about it tomorrow" Life!!!(JD) the philosopher

|172| "It takes a lot more time to heal a wound, than it takes to inflict a wound."(YVETTE CARNELL)

173| "Life doesn't always playout the way you expect." (Movie: THE MARKSMAN)

174| "You can learn from folks you disagree with." (DR CORNELL WEST)

175| "ONE'S GROWTH IS NOT MEASURED BY THE THINGS ONE POSSESS ONLY, BUT ALSO BY THE THINGS ONE DISCARD."(JD) the philosopher

176| "WE MUST NEVER CONFUSE CHARITY WITH JUSTICE."(DR CORNEL WEST)

177| "Reduction is to put your value on sale."(JAMAL BRYANT)

178| LOVE MATTERS! (JD) the philosopher

179| "A PHILOSOPHER IS A LOVER OF WISDOM."(DR CORNEL WEST)

180| "Real love is blind but it's true!"(JD) the philosopher

181| "You get back what you give back! (QUINCY JONES)

182| "I never did one thing right in my life, not one you know that!" and that takes skill." (LONG KISS GOOD NIGHT)

183| "JUST GIVE ME A RAINBOW, FIREWORKS A MIRACLE, LOVE AND A SMILE."(JD) the philosopher

184| "TO SEARCH MEANS ONE BELIEVE IT EXIST AND WONDER MEANS ONE IS VOID OF A ANSWER TO RESOLVE."(JD) the philosopher

185| "NO ONE EVER HATES A RAINBOW IN THE SKY." (JD) the philosopher

186| "SOMETIMES WE FIND OUR DREAMS IN PLACES WE NEVER LOOKED."(JD) the philosopher

187| "I want to grow to be at peace with that which I cannot change." (ANITA WILLIAMS)

188| "A GIFT GOES FURTHER THAN SKILLS"(SHARON HOLMES) A THERAPIST

|189| "LOVE NEVER GIVES HATE THE OPPORTUNITY TO BREAK EVEN."(JD) the philosopher

— *I wrote this to the conscious community that has morals and keep score of themselves and their decisions.*

|190| "NEVER UNDERESTIMATE THE HEART OF A CHAMPION."(RUDY TOMJANOVICH)

|191| "IN VAIN, DO NOT IGNORE THE PAIN, GIVE IT PURPOSE!"(AMANDA GORMAN)

|192| "The main thing I want to do is not count the years of my life but pretty much count the life I put in my years."(DAVID.D. CLEMENT)

|193| "WHEN DESIRE DIES, FEAR IS BORN."(GRECIAN)

|94| "WEALTH IS NOT THE BARRIER WHICH KEEP ONE FROM ACHIEVEMENT BUT THE WALL OF FEAR!"(SHARON HOLMES)

|95| "(MUSIC) HAS NO COLOR, BUT YOU GOT TO BE COLORFUL"(MIKE DAVIS)

> — *This was a statement that my coworker would say to me during a deep discussion on his favorite subject and perspective on the miracle of MUSIC!*

|96| "People fear what they don't understand and hate what they can't conquer"(ANDREW SMITH)

|97| "Sometimes you may lose some battles but win the war"(JD) the philosopher

|98| "Love is the bridge between you and everything"(RUMI)

199| "FALLING DOWN IS NOT FAILURE.FAILURE COMES WHEN YOU STAY WHERE YOU HAVE FALLEN"(SOCRATES)

200| "Time heals what reason cannot" (SENECA)

201| "I HAVE OFTEN REGRETED MY SPEECH, NEVER MY SILENCE"(XENOCRATES)

202| "YOU HAVE TO GET YOUR VALUE FROM WHO YOU ARE, AND NOT WHAT YOU DO"(JOEL OSTEEN)

203| "NOTHING BUILDS YOUR FAITH LIKE An ANSWERED PRAYER"(HAROLD JAMEAU)

— *This was a statement that was ordered by a wise man of his conclusion of the joy of being not being neglected of your desires by the Highest Power of mankind.*

204| "STRENGTHEN A MAN'S HANDS AND IT STRENGTHEN'S A MAN'S HEART"(JD) the philosopher

— *This was a statement that was made after a very popular Music icon father was recorded by his son when he was in a fit of rage that he had no idea of being on tape which many people were made aware of, and made judgements but I looked beyond what was said by the father and look at the fact of how special parents are and that everything they do, the children of a superstars heart are the benefactors of their strengthen hands of provision because they are their heart.*

205| "A BIRD IN THE HAND IS WORTH TWO IN THE BUSH"(ANCIENT PROVERB)\

206| "Love is always the best language to speak"(JD) the philosopher

207| "TO BE YOURSELF IN A WORLD THAT IS CONSTANTLY TRYING TO MAKE YOU SOMETHING ELSE IS THE GREATEST ACCOMPLISHMENT"(RALPH EMERSON)

208| "It's hard to fake ATTRACTION!"(DR TRACIE MARKS)

209| "We all require and want respect, man or woman, black or white, It's our basic human rights"(ARETHA FRANKLIN)

210| "Usually with judgement comes criticism"(DR TRACY MARKS)

211| "NEVER LEAVE THAT TILL TOMORROW WHICH YOU CAN DO TODAY"(BENJAMIN FRANKLIN)

212| "ALWAYS REMAIN THE BEST VERSION OF YOURSELF"(WAYNE DYER)

213| "MEASURE TWICE, CUT ONCE!"(JOHN FLORIO)

214| "NEVER ALLOW HOW YOU FEEL TO BE A REAL INDICATION OF WHO YOU REALLY ARE"(JD) the philosopher

— *I wrote this statement based on people that judge their mistakes and hasty emotion on them as a person, but your feelings never reflect how you are as the loving person.*

215| "THREE THINGS CANNOT BE LONG HIDDEN: THE SUN, THE MOON, AND THE TRUTH"(BUDDHA)

216| "When purpose is not known Abuse is Inevitable!"(MYLES MUNROE)

217| "STRENGTH DOES'T COME FROM WHAT YOU DO, IT COMES FROM OVERCOMING THE THINGS YOU ONCE THOUGHT YOU COULDN'T"(RIKKI ROGERS)

218| "MAN CONQUERS THE WORLD BY CONQUERING HIMSELF"(ZENO OF CITUM)

219| "LOVE CAN LEAVE PREGNANT WITH ONLY HOPE BUT RETURN CARRYING DESTINY"(JD) the philosopher

— *This is purely an ambiguous statement that gives the journey of being pushed away because of perception and bad judgment of people but some not seeing the full picture of destiny's children.*

220| "Change your life today. Don't gamble on the future. act now and without delay"(Simone de Beauvoir)

221| "WEALTH IS THE SLAVE OF THE WISE AND THE MASTER OF THE FOOL"(SENECA)

222| "WHEN A MAN'S HAND IS STRENGTHEN, HIS HEART IS ALSO STRENGTHEN!"(JD) THE PHILOSOPHER

223| GIVE MAN A FISH, AND YOU FEED HIM FOR A DAY. TEACH A MAN TO FISH, AND YOU FEED HIM FOR A LIFETIME"(CONFUCIUS)

224| "WE NEED TO LEARN MORE RESPONSIBILITY WITH THE POWER OF HAVING A VOICE" (ERIC LASALLE)

225| "I think that everything gets better"(EDDIE MURPHY)

226| "THESE ARE THE TIMES THAT TRY MEN'S SOUL."(THOMAS PAINE)

227| "EVERY GREAT DREAM BEGINS WITH A DREAMER ALWAYS REMEMBER THAT"(Harriet Tubman)

228| "I FEEL THAT THERE IS NOTHING MORE TRULY ARTISTIC THAN TO LOVE PEOPLE"(Vincent Van G)

229| "THERE IS NOTHING WRONG WITH GIVING"(Jim Thorpe)

230| "FOOTBALL IS JUST A GAME. WHAT MATTERS IS WHAT YOU PLAY FOR"(Ernie Davis)

231| "WHEN THERE IS NO REAL CLOSURE: THERE IS NO TRUE PEACE!"(JD) the philosopher

— *I wrote this concerning how that from experience the reason true peace exist in our life is because we have closure on the things that perplex us in all walks of life.*

232| "LAUGHTER IS TIMELESS!"(JD) the philosopher

233| "REAL LOVE SUSTAINS A MAN WHERE FALSE DREAMS AND AMBITIONS FAIL."(JD) the philosopher

234| "Well with the great depression just like every crisis there is a opportunity."(David Eisenach)

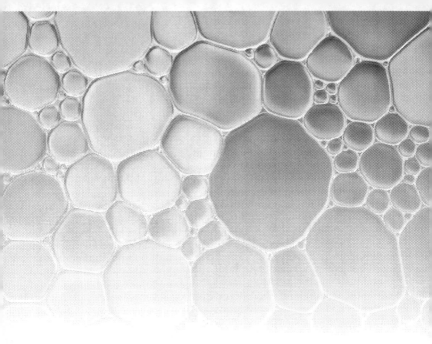

235| "TWO WRONGS DON'T MAKE A RIGHT."(MARCUS LOCKLAN)

236| "WE HAVE LEARNED THAT (QUIET!) ISN'T JUST ALWAYS (PEACE!)"(AMANDA GORMAN)

237| "I ADVOCATE BECAUSE I AM A VICTIM, BUT I AM A HERO BECAUSE I ADVOCATE."(JD) the philosopher

> — *I wrote this because most people that protest in any kind of matter whether Good or bad or happy or sad the reason in behind the reason of speaking out and forwardness is because we were a victim of the cause we now confront as well as any injustices in our lives and others.*

238| "WE HAVE LEARNED THAT (QUIET!) ISN'T JUST ALWAYS (PEACE!)"(AMANDA GORMAN)

239| "ONE IS NEVER TRULY ACTIVATED UNTIL ONE HAS EXPERIENCED BEING VIOLATED"(JD) the philosopher

240| "WITH INEXPERIENCE COMES FEAR, BUT WITH EXPERIENCE COMES CONFIDENCE AND COURAGE."(JD) the philosopher

241| "WE CAN SPEND TIME TRYING TO MAKE SENSE OF THINGS THAT DON'T MAKE SENSE OR ACCEPT SOMETHINGS WILL NEVER MAKE SENSE"(SHARON HOLMES)

— *This was spoken by a conversation between two sisters, and one being perplexed because of people's decisions with no change to the right resolve and the response of one helping the other sister understand and being ok with life not always making sense but learning to be ok with no resolve and grow off the things in life that offers resolve.*

242| "Love is the bridge between you and everything"(RUMI)

243| "People fear what they don't understand and hate what they can't conquer"(ANDREW SMITH)

244| "LOVE FIXES US IN WAYS THAT BROKEN PROMISES CANNOT"(JD) the philosopher

245| "ONE EITHER CHANGES TO FIT THE ENVIRONMENT OR EITHER CHANGES THE ENVIRONMENT TO FIT ONE"(JD) the philosopher

— *I wrote this inspired by the genius of the late artist PRINCE the singer musician and performer never conforming to the norm of artist and music but rather kept being his unique self and painting the world purple to accept his brand and his vision across the world.*

246| "NEVER ALLOW HOW YOU FEEL TO BE A TRUE INDICATION OF WHO YOU REALLY ARE"(JD) the philosopher

247| "LIFE IS SO MUCH SIMPLER WHEN YOU STOP EXPLAINING YOURSELF TO PEOPLE AND JUST DO WHAT WORKS FOR YOU" (RUMI)

248| "YOU LEARN NOTHING FROM LIFE IF YOU THINK YOU ARE RIGHT ALL THE TIME"(GAUTAMA BUDDHA)

249| "WHAT A MAN FEARS IS A GREAT INDICATION OF WHAT A MAN BELIEVES"(JD) the philosopher

— *I wrote this like one mentioned earlier about the truth and the concept of what many fear is based off what you tend to believe in.*

250| "WHAT A MAN BELIEVES SUSTAINS HIM BECAUSE IT SURPASSES WHAT HE FEEL"(JD) the philosopher

251| "ALWAYS REMAIN THE BEST VERSION OF YOURSELF"(WAYNE DYER)

252| "NEVER LEAVE THAT TILL TOMORROW WHICH YOU CAN DO TODAY"(BENJAMIN FRANKLIN)

253| "Today's wisdom was yesterday's Folly"(THOMAS DEXTER JAKES SR)

254| "LET THE BEAUTY OF WHAT YOU LOVE, BE WHAT YOU DO"(RUMI)

255| "WE SUFFER MORE OFTEN IN IMAGINATION THEN IN REALITY"(SENECA)

256| "WEALTH IS THE SLAVE OF THE WISE AND THE MASTER OF THE FOOL"(SENECA)

257| "LOVE THE LIFE YOU LIVE, LIVE THE LIFE YOU LOVE!"(BOB MARLEY)

258| A man's Greatest kept secret is what he fears"(JD) the philosopher

— *I wrote this as a general statement of the things many people keep hidden about the things, we all fear to protect our person which is normal.*

259| "Change your life today. Don't gamble on the future. act now and without delay"(Simone de Beauvoir)

260| "LUCK IS WHAT HAPPENS WHEN PREPARATION MEETS OPPORTUITY" (SENNECA)

261| "I have to remind myself that some birds aren't meant to be caged"(Shawshank Redemption)

262| "Tell me and I forget, teach me and I remember, involve me and I learn!"(Benjamin Franklin)

263| "WHEN THE DEBATE IS OVER, SLANDER BECOMES THE TOOL OF THE LOOSER"(SOCRATES)

264| "EMPOWERING WOMEN ISN'T JUST THE RIGHT THING TO DO-ITS THE SMART THING TO DO!"(BARACK OBAMA)

265| "CHANGE WILL NOT COME IF WE WAIT FOR SOME OTHER PERSON OR SOME OTHER TIME"(BARACK OBAMA)

266| "REAL FIGHTERS DON'T COMPLAIN AND REAL COMPLAINERS DON'T FIGHT"(JD) the philosopher

— *I wrote this concerning people that use the obsessive method of complaining about problem we face instead of concentrating on solving and changing the outcome of their perplexities.*

267| "ACTION IS THE FOUNDATIONAL KEY TO ALL SUCCESS"(PABLO PICASSO)

268| "Release you! because you are the premier and the world has been waiting on you!"(JD) the philosopher

269| "I REALLY WANT YOU TO DIE EMPTY, DIE FINISHED"(MILES MUNROE)

270| "Do not let what you cannot do interfere with what you can do"(JOHN WOODEN)

271| "SOME GREAT MEN ARE FAMOUS FOR THINGS GAINED BUT SOME GOOD MEN ARE HERO'S FOR THINGS SACRIFICED"(JD) the philosopher

> — *I wrote this inspired by famous men and women that are UNSUNG because they seen sacrifice as gain and not sacrifice as lost because they seen the bigger picture of self-sacrifice and its rewards.*

272| "YOU CAN TEACH KNOWLEDGE BUT YOU CAN NOT TEACH WISDOM"(KEITH DAVIS)

> — *This was mentioned to me by a man that believed there is something's you can't teach as curriculum learning; they are given by a greater source that no man can teach which is WISDOM.*

273| "I am not afraid of failure but rather the loneliness of regret"(JD) the philosopher

274| "THOSE WHO DO NOT REMEMBER THE PAST ARE CONDEMNED TO REPEAT IT" (GEORGE SANTAYANA)

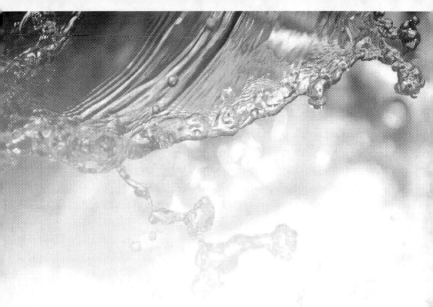

275| "When one shed's his own blood it's a sign that one is truly human."(JD) the philosopher

276| "IF YOU HAVE TO PURCHASE THE TRUTH YOU PROBABLY PAID A LIE" (JD) the philosopher

277| "BETTER THE CHANCES OF THE WISE THAN THE CHOICES OF FOOLS."(JD) the philosopher

278| "THE BELLS THAT RING THE SWEETEST OF SONG ALWAYS CHIME A FAMILIAR MELODY." (JD) the philosopher

279| "LOVE MAKES LIFE WORTH LIVING."(JD) the philosopher

280| "SOMETIMES WE FIND OUR DREAMS IN PLACES WE NEVER LOOKED."(JD) the philosopher

— *I wrote this inspired by the fact that many people lend their gifts to what is popular only to find themselves not looking within their heart in the place that has been calling them all their life that is true.*

281| "REAL STRENGTH IS NOT USING YOUR POWER BUT SHOWING YOUR LOVE."(JD) the philosopher

282| "PURE HEARTS BELIEVE IN LOVE TOO! AND SOFT EARS HEAR MELODIES AND BABIES CAN SEE RAINBOWS."(JD) the philosopher

283| "REAL LOVE SUSTAINS A MAN WHERE FALSE DREAMS AND AMBITIONS FAIL."(JD) the philosopher

284| "LOVE NEVER APOLOGIZE FOR BEING TRUE, THE SKY NEVER APOLOGIZE FOR BEING BLUE, SO NEVER APOLOGIZE FOR BEING YOU." (JD) the philosopher

285| "With confidence you have won before you have started"(MARCUS GARVEY)

286| "KNOWLEDGE SPEAKS BUT WISDOM LISTENS"(JIMI HENDRIX)

287| "PATIENCE IS BITTER BUT THE FRUIT IS SWEET"(ARISTOTLE)

288| "THAT WHICH DOES NOT KILL US MAKES US STRONGER"(NEECHE)

289| "Whatever the mind perceives, it makes real"(KRS ONE)

290| "I like a man that achieve his goals and makes all his dreams come true for himself and for the people"(Michael Jackson)

291| "HOPE IS THERAPY WITHIN ITSELF"(ANITA DAVIS)

292| "PEOPLE DON'T CARE HOW MUCH YOU KNOW UNTIL THEY KNOW HOW MUCH YOU CARE"(THEODORE ROOSEVELT)

— *I heard my sister who is a therapist talking with my other sister who is also a therapist on the conversation of their professional field while conversating around the house.*

293| "The reason one succeeds is because one doesn't know that one is not supposed to succeed." (JD) the philosopher

294| "TO QUOTE SOMEONE IS A SIGN THAT WE ARE LISTENING"(JD) the philosopher

295| "REMEMBER IN THIS RACE WE DON'T PASS TORCHES BUT WE PASS BATONS BECAUSE WE ARE ALL IN THIS TOGETHER!" (JD) the philosopher

— *I wrote this in 2020 during the lock down as a way of paying tribute to the many people making sacrifices and for a good and worthy cause which it shows the hearts of AMERICANS and their resilience and love for one another during such a trying time in America.*

296| "The two most important days in your life are the day you are born and the day you find out why."(MARK TWAIN)

297| "EXPOSING ONE'S VULNERABILITIES ALLOWS OTHERS TO DISCOVER ONE'S TRUE ABILITIES"(JD) the philosopher

298| "Sometimes one has to get it Wrong to get it Right and Start it to Finish it and Abuse it to Quit it and Lose it to Win it"(JD)

— *I wrote this inspired by the hard fight in people that has push to rally themselves even being faced with outstanding odds and struggles that shows its not the size of the MAN fighting but the size of the FIGHT in the man, so you just keep on pushing people and if you fall you get back up again.*

299| "CRY ABOUT IT NOW AND LAUGH AT IT LATER OR LAUGH AT IT NOW AND CRY ABOUT IT LATER"(JD) THE PHILOSOPHER

— *I wrote this for the many people across the world that feel bad about even present mistakes and tears that are shed and the feeling that there is no hope but to remember just because we cry about it today we will come to laugh at it tomorrow but on the flip side people that enjoy a laugh at someone's pain may come to regret their future decisions that will prove to be future pain in disguise.*

300| "OFTEN TIMES DESTINY HAS TO DISABLE US FOR LOVE TO ABLE US"(JD) the philosopher

301| "I love art because art helps us to envision a new world"(JOHN LEGEND)

302| "WHEN ONE'S DREAM IS TAKEN, ANOTHER DREAM IS BORN"(JD) THE PHILOSOPHER

303| "LADIES AND GENTLE MEN THE RISE OF THE POETS AND PHILOSOPHERS HAS BEGUN!"(JD) the philosopher

304| "The Hand that rocks the cradle is the Hand that rules the World"(William Ross Wallace)

305| "WE CHOOSE MANY THINGS IN LIFE BUT THERE ARE THINGS IN LIFE THAT CHOOSE US"(JD) the philosopher

306| "NOTHING BEATS A FAILURE BUT A TRY"(R.J. SMITH)

307| "We make no excuse for what we have, for this that we have the Lord has provided and we are thankful"(ELIZABETH COOK)

308| "Things always work out best, to him that makes the best out of the way things work out"(John Wooten)

309| "Give me Liberty or Give me Death"(Patrick Matthew)

310| "ITS NOT ABOUT HAVING SOMETHING TO HIDE BUT ABOUT HAVING SOMETHING TO SAY"(TARAJI P HENSON)

311| "SOME DESIRES AND EMOTIONS ARE A BYPRODUCT OF A BIGGER PROBLEM"(JD) the philosopher

— *I wrote this really understanding the human science in behind the things we as people are ashamed of in our lives that if we would look further into ours and other actions, we would find the answers that explain the reason and decisions we make.*

312| "BE INTENTIONAL TO WIN BUT THYSELF TO COMPETE"(JD) the philosopher

313| The only true competitor in an infinite game is yourself. (TERRY VOLPATTI)

314| Excitement comes from the achievement; Fulfillment comes from the journey that got you there (TERRY VOLPATTI)

315| "A mentor is not someone who walks ahead of us to show us how they did it, A mentor walks along side us to show us what we can do." (TERRY VOLPATTI)

316| "The value of learning is greater when we share what we learn." (TERRY VOLPATTI)

317| "Building trust requires nothing more than telling the truth." (TERRY VOLPATTI)

318| Sometimes it is the people NO ONE CAN IMAGINE anything of who do the things NO ONE CAN IMAGINE. (ALAN TURING)

319| Instead of expending energy to fit into the group, it's better to expend energy to find the group in which we fit. (TERRY VOLPATTI)

Printed in the United States
by Baker & Taylor Publisher Services